# THE TREA
## *Charles*

### SELECTED WRITINGS

**BARBOUR**
PUBLISHING

© 2004 by Barbour Publishing, Inc.

ISBN 1-59310-238-0

Compiled by Dan Harmon.

This book was excerpted from the title *Treasures from Charles Spurgeon,* © 1998 by Barbour Publishing, Inc.

Cover image © Photo Disc

Scripture quotations are taken from the King James Version of the Bible.

Published by Barbour Publishing, Inc., P.O. Box 719, Uhrichsville, Ohio 44683, www.barbourbooks.com

*Our mission is to publish and distribute inspirational products offering exceptional value and biblical encouragement to the masses.*

 Member of the
Evangelical Christian
Publishers Association

Printed in the United States of America.
5 4 3 2 1

# Introduction

"I looked at God,
and He looked at me,
and we were one forever."

CHARLES SPURGEON

His life was not long, but his legacy remains more than a century after his death. Charles Haddon Spurgeon, one of the best-known preachers of all time, died in 1892 at the age of fifty-seven after shepherding huge congregations in England and leaving extensive writings to posterity.

Though he was known as a great orator, Spurgeon's words also have tremendous power on the printed page. More than sixty volumes of his sermons were published in book form between 1855 and 1917, and Spurgeon penned other books, as well, including the popular devotional *Morning & Evening*. Constantly encouraging, challenging, and interesting, Spurgeon's thoughts continue to spur Christians on to a greater love for and commitment to Christ and His Word.

This book, *The Treasures of Charles Spurgeon*, contains gems of truth drawn from Spurgeon's many works, each organized by topic and accompanied by a relevant Bible verse. You'll find your heart stirred by the godly passion of Charles Spurgeon, and your thoughts drawn to the Lord he loved and served.

# Contents

# Age

Remember now thy Creator
in the days of thy youth,
while the evil days come not,
nor the years draw nigh,
when thou shalt say,
I have no pleasure in them.

ECCLESIASTES 12:1

Oh, it is sweet to come to Christ
in the early morning of life,
to have a long day of happiness before you!

Cast me not off in the time of old age;
forsake me not when my strength faileth.

PSALM 71:9

Frail flowers of the field,
we must not reckon upon
blooming forever.
There is a time appointed for
weakness and sickness,
when we shall have to
glorify God by suffering,
and not by earnest activity.

# Atonement

With lovingkindness have I drawn thee.
JEREMIAH 31:3

What Moses with the tablets of stone
could never do,
Christ does with His pierced hand.
Such is the doctrine of effectual calling.

And that lord answered
the man of God, and said,
Now, behold, if the LORD should
make windows in heaven,
might such a thing be?
And he said,
Behold, thou shalt see it with thine eyes,
but shalt not eat thereof.
2 KINGS 7:19

There is an atonement made for
the unbelief of a Christian
because it is temporary;
but the final unbelief—
the unbelief with which men die—
never was atoned for.

# Awe of God

The heavens declare the glory of God;
and the firmament sheweth his handywork.

PSALM 19:1

It is humbling to find that even when
the most devout and elevated minds are
desirous to express their loftiest thoughts of God,
they must use words and metaphors
drawn from the earth.

His camp is very great.

JOEL 2:11

Consider, my soul,
the mightiness of the Lord who is
thy glory and defence.
He is a man of war, Jehovah is His name.
All the forces of heaven are at His beck,
legions wait at His door,
cherubim and seraphim;
watchers and holy ones,
principalities and powers,
are all attentive to His will.

# Backsliding

The backslider in heart shall be
filled with his own ways:
and a good man shall be
satisfied from himself.

PROVERBS 14:14

Every little backsliding, as men call it,
is a great mischief;
every little going back even in heart from God
if it never comes to words or deeds,
yet will involve us in some measure of sorrow.

Only take heed to thyself,
and keep thy soul diligently,
lest thou forget the things which
thine eyes have seen,
and lest they depart from thy heart
all the days of thy life.

DEUTERONOMY 4:9

Leave off going forward
and you will slide backward,
cease going upward
and you will go downward of necessity;
for stand still you never can.

# Blessings

Who hath blessed us with
all spiritual blessings. . .
EPHESIANS 1:3

All the goodness of the past,
the present, and the future,
Christ bestows upon His people.

Thou crownest the year with thy goodness.
PSALM 65:11

All the year round, every hour of every day,
God is richly blessing us;
both when we sleep and when we wake
His mercy waits upon us.

God, even our own God. . .
PSALM 67:6

It is strange how little use we make of
the spiritual blessings which God gives us,
but it is stranger still how little use
we make of God Himself.

# Burdens

On him they laid the cross,
that he might bear it after Jesus.

LUKE 23:26

But let us comfort ourselves with this thought,
that in our case, as in Simon's, it is not our cross,
but Christ's cross which we carry.

The iron did swim.

2 KINGS 6:6

Beloved reader, what is thy desperate case?
What heavy matter hast thou in hand this evening?
Bring it hither.

For as the sufferings of Christ abound in us,
so our consolation also aboundeth by Christ.

2 CORINTHIANS 1:5

There is no cry so good as that which
comes from the bottom of the mountains;
no prayer half so hearty as that which
comes up from the depths of the soul,
through deep trials and afflictions.

# Church

Tell his disciples that
he is risen from the dead;
and, behold,
he goeth before you into Galilee;
there shall ye see him.

MATTHEW 28:7

There, in Galilee,
is the place where Jesus will hold
the first general assembly of His church
after His resurrection.

Upon this rock I will build my church;
and the gates of hell
shall not prevail against it.

MATTHEW 16:18

Ah! but the worst harvest will be that of those
who sin against the church of Christ. . . .
He that touches one of God's people,
touches the apple of His eye.

# Communion with God

Abide in me.

JOHN 15:4

Communion with Christ is
a certain cure for every ill.

❧

Your heavenly Father. . .

MATTHEW 6:26

Abba, Father! He who can say this,
hath uttered better music than
cherubim or seraphim can reach.
There is heaven in the depth of that word—
Father! . . . I have all in all
to all eternity when I can say, "Father."

❧

And I looked,
and, lo,
a Lamb stood on the mount Sion.

REVELATION 14:1

To be with Christ is to be in heaven,
and to be in heaven is to be with Christ.

# Community of Christians

Let us not sleep, as do others.

I THESSALONIANS 5:6

Christians who isolate themselves and walk alone,
are very liable to grow drowsy.
Hold Christian company,
and you will be kept wakeful by it,
and refreshed and encouraged to make
quicker progress in the road to heaven.

And all ye are brethren.

MATTHEW 23:8

There is nothing which happens
to one member of society which
does not affect all.

A companion of fools shall be destroyed.

PROVERBS 13:20

Keep the best company. . . .
Let them be thy choicest
companions who have made Christ
their choicest companion.

# Contentment

I have learned, in whatsoever state I am,
therewith to be content.

PHILIPPIANS 4:11

These words show us that contentment is not
a natural propensity of man. . . .
Covetousness, discontent, and murmuring
are as natural to man as thorns are to the soil.

Rest in the LORD, and wait patiently for him.

PSALM 37:7

Contentment is one of the flowers of heaven,
and if we would have it, it must be cultivated;
it will not grow in us by nature;
it is the new nature alone that can produce it.

As God hath distributed to every man,
as the Lord hath called every one,
so let him walk.

1 CORINTHIANS 7:17

When our Father does not give us more,
we should be content with His daily allowance.

And his allowance was a
continual allowance given him of the king,
a daily rate for every day,
all the days of his life.

2 Kings 25:30

A daily portion is all that a man really wants.
We do not need tomorrow's supplies;
that day has not yet dawned,
and its wants are as yet unborn.
The thirst which we may suffer
in the month of June does not need to
be quenched in February,
for we do not feel it yet;
if we have enough for each day
as the days arrive we shall never know want.

God is our refuge and strength,
a very present help in trouble.

Psalm 46:1

When waves of distress,
and billows of affliction pass over the Christian,
there are times when his faith is so strong
that he lies down and sleeps,
though the hurricane is thundering in his ears. . . .
He says, "God is our refuge and strength,
a very present help in trouble."

19

# Courage

Then all the disciples forsook him,
and fled.

MATTHEW 26:56

Divine grace can make the coward brave.

And I give unto them eternal life;
and they shall never perish.

JOHN 10:28

Christian!
it is contrary to every promise of
God's precious Word
that thou shouldst ever be forgotten
or left to perish.

Be strong, and of good courage;
dread not, nor be dismayed.

1 CHRONICLES 22:13

Who wants to paddle about
in a duck pond all his life?
Launch out into the deep.

# Covenant

He hath commanded his covenant for ever.
PSALM 111:9

The Lord's people delight in the covenant itself. . . .
They delight to contemplate
the antiquity of that covenant,
remembering that before the day-star knew its place,
or planets ran their round,
the interests of the saints were
made secure in Christ Jesus. . . .
The covenant is a treasury of wealth, a granary of food,
a fountain of life, a store-house of salvation,
a charter of peace, and a haven of joy.

And I will remember my covenant.
GENESIS 9:15

Oh! It is not my remembering God,
it is God's remembering me which is
the ground of my safety;
it is not my laying hold of His covenant,
but His covenant's laying hold on me.

# Death

I pray not that thou shouldest
take them out of the world.

JOHN 17:15

It is a sweet and blessed event which will occur
to all believers in God's own time—
the going home to be with Jesus.

Them also which sleep in Jesus
will God bring with him.

1 THESSALONIANS 4:14

Blessed is death, since it,
through the divine power,
disrobes us of this work-day garment,
to clothe us with
the wedding garment of incorruption.

The things which are not seen. . .

2 CORINTHIANS 4:18

Hush, hush, my doubts!
death is but a narrow stream,
and thou shalt soon have forded it.

And they heard a great voice from heaven
saying unto them, Come up hither.

REVELATION 11:12

We are not called down to the grave,
but up to the skies.

She called his name Ben-oni [son of sorrow]:
but his father called him Benjamin
[son of my right hand].

GENESIS 35:18

When death itself appears,
faith points to the light of
resurrection beyond the grave,
thus making our dying Benoni
to be our living Benjamin.

For the end of those things is death.

ROMANS 6:21

Thy soul's eternal state hangs on the turn of today.
Loiter thy time away, waste thine abilities,
take thy religion at second hand, of thy priest,
of thy minister, or of thy friend,
and in the next world thou shalt
everlastingly rue the error.

# Dependence on God

Into thine hand I commit my spirit:
thou hast redeemed me,
O LORD God of truth.

PSALM 31:5

At all times we should commit
our all to Jesus' faithful hand.

Jesus saith unto him,
I am the way, the truth, and the life:
no man cometh unto the Father, but by me.

JOHN 14:6

To be one of God's people,
the essential thing is a simple dependence
upon Jesus Christ.

Giving all diligence, add to your faith virtue.

2 PETER 1:5

Take care that thy faith is of the right kind—
that it is not a mere belief of doctrine,
but a simple faith, depending on Christ,
and on Christ alone.

# Despair

My God, my God,
why hast thou forsaken me?

PSALM 22:1

There are seasons when the brightness of our
Father's smile is eclipsed by clouds and darkness;
but let us remember that God
never does really forsake us.

Casting all your care upon him;
for he careth for you.

1 PETER 5:7

The blackest gloom shall give place to the morning.

I have exalted one chosen out of the people.

PSALM 89:19

However difficult and painful thy road,
it is marked by the footsteps of thy Saviour;
and even when thou reachest the dark valley of
the shadow of death,
and the deep waters of the swelling Jordan,
thou wilt find His footprints there.

# Discontent

And all the children of Israel murmured.

NUMBERS 14:2

There are murmurers amongst Christians now,
as there were in the camp of Israel of old.

The LORD hath done great things for us;
whereof we are glad.

PSALM 126:3

Some Christians are sadly prone to
look on the dark side of everything,
and to dwell more upon what
they have gone through than upon
what God has done for them.

And having food and raiment
let us be therewith content.

1 TIMOTHY 6:8

One staff aids a traveler,
but a bundle of staves is a heavy burden.
Enough is not only as good as a feast,
but is all that the veriest glutton can truly enjoy.

# Doubt

I will accept you with your sweet savour.

EZEKIEL 20:41

Notwithstanding all your doubts,
and fears, and sins,
Jehovah's gracious eye never looks
upon you in anger.

Then the eleven disciples
went away into Galilee,
into a mountain where
Jesus had appointed them.
And when they saw him,
they worshipped him:
but some doubted.

MATTHEW 28:16–17

We can never expect to be
quite free from doubters in the church,
since even in the presence of
the newly risen Christ,
"some doubted."

Behold, I have graven thee upon
the palms of my hands.
ISAIAH 49:16

We know not which most to wonder at,
the faithfulness of God or
the unbelief of His people.
He keeps His promise a thousand times,
and yet the next trial makes us doubt Him.

And he saith unto them, Why are ye fearful,
O ye of little faith?
MATTHEW 8:26

What are your doubts this morning?
Whatever they are,
they can find a kind and fond solution
here by looking at Christ on the cross.

Then Agrippa said unto Paul,
Almost thou persuadest me to be a Christian.
ACTS 26:28

And really I am convinced that
every Christian has his doubts at times
and that the people who do not doubt
are just the people that ought to doubt;
for he who never doubts about his state
perhaps may do so when it is too late.

# Election

Now we have received. . .
the spirit which is of God;
that we might know the things that are
freely given to us of God.

1 CORINTHIANS 2:12

What effect does the doctrine of election have
upon any man until the Spirit of God enters into him?
Election is a dead letter in my consciousness
until the Spirit of God calls me out of darkness
into marvelous light.
Then through my calling,
I see my election,
and knowing myself to be called of God,
I know myself to have been chosen
in the eternal purpose.

According as he hath chosen us in him
before the foundation of the world,
that we should be holy and
without blame before him in love.

EPHESIANS 1:4

There will be no doubt about His having chosen you,
when you have chosen Him.

# Envy

Let not thine heart envy sinners:
but be thou in the fear of the LORD all the day long.
For surely there is an end;
and thine expectation shall not be cut off.
PROVERBS 23:17–18

The cure for envy lies in living under
a constant sense of the divine presence,
worshiping God and communing with Him
all the day long.

If ye have bitter envying
and strife in your hearts,
glory not, and lie not against the truth.
JAMES 3:14

The more of heaven there is in our lives,
the less of earth we shall covet.

I. . .will be their God.
JEREMIAH 31:33

Dost thou want anything but God?

# Evangelism

And ye also shall bear witness,
because ye have been with me
from the beginning.

JOHN 15:27

Thou mayst or thou mayst not
be called to evangelize the people
in any particular locality,
but certainly thou art called to see
after thine own servants,
thine own kinsfolk and acquaintance.

Unto me, who am less than
the least of all saints,
is this grace given,
that I should preach among the Gentiles
the unsearchable riches of Christ.

EPHESIANS 3:8

The apostle Paul felt it a great privilege
to be allowed to preach the gospel.
He did not look upon his calling as a drudgery,
but he entered upon it with intense delight.

# Faith

Without faith it is
impossible to please him.

HEBREWS 11:6

There shall never be an acceptable offering
which has not been seasoned with faith.

This is the work of God,
that ye believe on him
whom he hath sent.

JOHN 6:29

The first thing in faith is knowledge.
A man cannot believe what he does not know.

Then Jesus answered and said unto her,
O woman, great is thy faith:
be it unto thee even as thou wilt.

MATTHEW 15:28

When I am perfect in faith,
I shall be perfect in everything else.

Dost thou believe on the Son of God?

JOHN 9:35

Virtues without faith are whitewashed sins;
obedience without faith,
if it is possible,
is a gilded disobedience.

If we live in the Spirit,
let us also walk in the Spirit.

GALATIANS 5:25

You will never find true faith
unattended by true godliness;
on the other hand,
you will never discover
a truly holy life which has not
for its root a living faith upon
the righteousness of Christ.

According to your faith be it unto you.

MATTHEW 9:29

We must have faith, for this is the foundation;
we must have holiness of life,
for this is the superstructure.

# Fear

And the angel answered
and said unto the women,
Fear not ye:
for I know that ye seek Jesus,
which was crucified.

MATTHEW 28:5

Only Jesus can silence
the fears of trembling hearts.

And Ananias hearing these words fell down,
and gave up the ghost:
and great fear came on all them
that heard these things.

ACTS 5:5

And you that fear death—
why fear to die?
Jesus died before you,
and He passed through the iron gates,
and as He passed them before you,
He will come and meet you.

# Goodness

The backslider in heart
shall be filled with his own ways:
and a good man shall be satisfied.

PROVERBS 14:14

All the good men I have ever met
have always wanted to be better.

It is a good thing that the heart
be established with grace.

HEBREWS 13:9

When a good man is enabled by
divine grace to live in obedience to God,
he must, as a necessary consequence,
enjoy peace of mind.

They have not set God before them.

PSALM 54:3

Good delayed is evil indulged.

# Grace

Have mercy upon me, O God.
PSALM 51:1

Only on the footing of free grace
can the most experienced
and most honoured of the saints
approach their God.

But Simon's wife's mother lay sick of a fever,
and anon they tell him of her.

MARK 1:30

Jesus is looking round your room now,
and is waiting to be gracious to you.

The free gift came upon all men
unto justification of life.
ROMANS 5:18

It is blessed to know that the grace of God
is free to us at all times,
without preparation, without fitness,
without money, and without price!

# Happiness

If thou believest with all thine heart,
thou mayest.

ACTS 8:37

When Jesus comes into the heart,
He issues a general license
to be glad in the Lord.

Therefore I take pleasure in infirmities,
in reproaches, in necessities,
in persecutions,
in distresses for Christ's sake:
for when I am weak,
then am I strong.

2 CORINTHIANS 12:10

Let us remember that the only way
to keep our life peaceful and happy
is to keep the heart at rest;
for come poverty, come wealth,
come honor, come shame,
come plenty, or come scarcity,
if the heart be quiet,
there will be happiness anywhere.

# Harvest

Is it not wheat harvest to day?

1 Samuel 12:17

In one sense the Christian is the seed,
in another he is a sower.
In one sense he is a seed sown
by God which is to grow,
and ripen, and germinate
till the great harvest time.
In another sense,
every Christian is a sower sent into the world
to sow good seed and to sow good seed only.

He reserveth unto us the appointed
weeks of the harvest.

Jeremiah 5:24

Every Christian has his harvest. . . .
But if you should not live to see it on earth,
remember you are only accountable for
your labor and not for your success.
Sow still, toil on!

# Heart

For the flesh lusteth against the Spirit,
and the Spirit against the flesh.

GALATIANS 5:17

In every believer's heart there is
a constant struggle between
the old nature and the new.

❧

And thou shalt love the LORD thy God
with all thine heart.

DEUTERONOMY 6:5

If thou desirest Christ for a perpetual guest,
give Him all the keys of thine heart;
let not one cabinet be locked up from Him. . . .

❧

Create in me a clean heart, O God;
and renew a right spirit within me.

PSALM 51:10

Jesus will never tarry in a divided heart.
He must be all or nothing.

# Holiness

And declared to be the Son of God with power,
according to the spirit of holiness,
by the resurrection from the dead. . .
ROMANS 1:4

The way to holiness is not through Moses
but through Christ.

And above all these things put on charity,
which is the bond of perfectness.

COLOSSIANS 3:14

If we were more like Christ,
we should be more ready to hope for the hopeless,
to value the worthless,
and to love the depraved.

Godliness is profitable unto all things,
having promise of the life that now is,
and of that which is to come.
1 TIMOTHY 4:8

Get right within, and you will be right without.

Yea, a man may say, Thou hast faith,
and I have works:
shew me thy faith without thy works,
and I will shew thee my faith by my works.

JAMES 2:18

If a man says he has faith and
has no works, he lies;
if any man declares that he believes on Christ
and yet does not lead a holy life,
he makes a mistake;
for while we do not trust in good works,
we know that faith always begets good works.

The highway of the upright is
to depart from evil.

PROVERBS 16:17

Periodical godliness is perpetual hypocrisy.

Ye cannot drink the cup of the Lord,
and the cup of devils:
ye cannot be partakers of the Lord's table,
and of the table of devils.

1 CORINTHIANS 10:21

Saintly souls should not be lodged in filthy bodies.

# Hope

They looked unto him, and were lightened:
and their faces were not ashamed.
PSALM 34:5

Make Christ the only pillar of your hope
and never seek to buttress or prop Him up.

 ❧

The hope which is
laid up for you in heaven. . .
COLOSSIANS 1:5

Our hope in Christ for the future is
the mainspring and the mainstay of our joy here.
It will animate our hearts to think often of heaven,
for all that we can desire is promised there.

 ❧

Shew me wherefore
thou contendest with me.
JOB 10:2

Hope itself is like a star—
not to be seen in the sunshine of prosperity,
and only to be discovered in the night of adversity.

# Humility

Be clothed with humility:
for God resisteth the proud,
and giveth grace to the humble.

1 PETER 5:5

God has seldom chosen
the great men of this world.
High places and faith
in Christ do seldom agree.

A living dog is better than a dead lion.

ECCLESIASTES 9:4

It is better to be the least in
the kingdom of heaven than the greatest out of it.
The lowest degree of grace is superior to
the noblest development of unregenerate nature.

Behold, if the leprosy have covered all his flesh,
he shall pronounce him clean that hath the plague.

LEVITICUS 13:13

Nothing is more deadly than self-righteousness,
or more hopeful than contrition.

Behold, what manner of love the Father
hath bestowed upon us,
that we should be called the sons of God:
therefore the world knoweth us not,
because it knew him not.
Beloved, now are we the sons of God.

1 JOHN 3:1–2

We are content to be unknown with Him
in His humiliation,
for we are to be exalted with Him.

Grow in grace, and in the knowledge of
our Lord and Saviour Jesus Christ.

2 PETER 3:18

Seek to lie very low,
and know more of your own nothingness.

The four and twenty elders fall down
before him that sat on the throne,
and worship him that liveth for ever and ever,
and cast their crowns before the throne.

REVELATION 4:10

Think not that humility is weakness;
it shall supply the marrow of strength to thy bones.
Stoop and conquer; bow thyself and become invincible.

# Indebtedness to God

Son of man,
what is the vine tree more than any tree,
or than a branch which is among
the trees of the forest?

EZEKIEL 15:2

The more thou hast,
the more thou art in debt to God;
and thou shouldst not be proud of
that which renders thee a debtor.

Who can understand his errors?
cleanse thou me from secret faults.

PSALM 19:12

Great believer,
thou wouldst have been a great sinner
if God had not made thee to differ.

Therefore, brethren, we are debtors.

ROMANS 8:12

Consider how much you owe to His forgiving grace,
that after ten thousand affronts
He loves you as infinitely as ever.

# Inerrancy of Scripture

Go ye therefore, and teach all nations,
baptizing them in the name of the Father,
and of the Son, and of the Holy Ghost:
Teaching them to observe all things
whatsoever I have commanded you.

MATTHEW 28:19–20

We are not to invent anything new,
nor to change anything to suit
the current of the age,
but to teach the baptized believers to observe
"all things whatsoever"
our Divine King has commanded.

The law of the LORD is perfect,
converting the soul:
the testimony of the LORD
is sure, making wise the simple.

PSALM 19:7

The gospel is perfect in all its parts,
and perfect as a whole:
it is a crime to add to it,
treason to alter it,
and felony to take from it.

# Joy in Christ

Delight thyself also in the LORD.
PSALM 37:4

The thought of delight in religion
is so strange to most men,
that no two words in their language stand
further apart than "holiness" and "delight."
But believers who know Christ,
understand that delight and faith
are so blessedly united,
that the gates of hell cannot
prevail to separate them.

Whosoever drinketh of the water
that I shall give him
shall never thirst.
JOHN 4:14

The believer is not the man whose days are
weary for want of comfort,
and whose nights are long from
absence of heart-cheering thought,
for he finds in religion such a spring of joy,
such a fountain of consolation,
that he is content and happy.

# Judgment

The LORD is slow to anger,
and great in power.

NAHUM 1:3

God marketh His enemies,
and yet He bestirs not Himself,
but holdeth in His anger.

With lovingkindness have I drawn thee.

JEREMIAH 31:3

The thunders of the law and
the terrors of judgment are
all used to bring us to Christ;
but the final victory is
effected by lovingkindness.

Therefore, brethren, we are debtors.

ROMANS 8:12

I am a debtor to God's grace and forgiving mercy;
but I am no debtor to His justice,
for He will never accuse me of
a debt already paid.

# Knowing God

Get thee up into the high mountain.

ISAIAH 40:9

When we first believe in Christ
we see but little of Him.
The higher we climb the more we
discover of His beauties.

Moreover by them is thy servant warned:
and in keeping of them there is great reward.

PSALM 19:11

Oh, the glory yet to be revealed!

He that loveth me shall be loved of my Father,
and I will love him,
and will manifest myself to him.

JOHN 14:21

We now see that to know Christ is to love Him.
It is impossible to have a vision of His face,
to behold His person, or understand His offices,
without feeling our souls warmed towards Him.

Thou whom my soul loveth. . .

SONG OF SOLOMON 1:7

Get positive knowledge of your love of Jesus,
and be not satisfied till you can speak of
your interest in Him as a reality.

That I may know him,
and the power of his resurrection,
and the fellowship of his sufferings,
being made conformable unto his death;
if by any means I might attain
unto the resurrection of the dead.

PHILIPPIANS 3:10–11

We should, as good traders in heaven's market,
covet to be enriched in the knowledge of Jesus.

Grow in grace, and in the knowledge
of our Lord and Saviour Jesus Christ.

2 PETER 3:18

He who does not long to know more of Christ,
knows nothing of Him yet.

# *Love*

Thou shalt love thy neighbour.
MATTHEW 5:43

Take heed that thou love thy neighbour
even though he be in rags,
or sunken in the depths of poverty.

Remember the poor.
GALATIANS 2:10

If we truly love Christ,
we shall care for those who are loved by Him.

Husbands, love your wives,
even as Christ also loved the church.
EPHESIANS 5:25

The Christian should take nothing short of
Christ for his model.
Under no circumstances ought we to be content
unless we reflect the grace which was in Him.

# *Love of Jesus*

I will. . .
give thee for a covenant of the people.

ISAIAH 49:8

Has He love?
Well, there is not a drop of love
in His heart which is not yours;
you may dive into the immense ocean of His love,
and you may say of it all, "It is mine."

What man of you,
having an hundred sheep,
if he lose one of them,
doth not leave the ninety
and nine in the wilderness,
and go after that which is lost,
until he find it?

LUKE 15:4

Every step is hard for the Shepherd.
He must tread painfully
all that length of road over which
the sheep had wandered so wantonly.
The sheep is carried back with
no suffering on its own part.

As the Father hath loved me,
so have I loved you:
continue ye in my love.

JOHN 15:9

The love of Jesus is not mere sentiment;
it is active and energetic.

I will; be thou clean.

MARK 1:41

The love of Jesus is the source of salvation.
He loves, He looks, He touches us, We Live.

The love of the LORD. . .

HOSEA 3:1

Surely as we meditate on "the love of the LORD,"
our hearts burn within us,
and we long to love Him more.

The place, which is called Calvary.

LUKE 23:33

He who would know love, let him retire to Calvary and
see the Man of Sorrows die.

# Ministers

Beware of false prophets,
which come to you in sheep's clothing,
but inwardly they are ravening wolves.

MATTHEW 7:15

He must be clean who ministers at the altar.

                        Can the blind lead the blind?

LUKE 6:39

Happy the church when God gives her holy ministers;
but unhappy the church where wicked men preside.

There is a conspiracy of
her prophets in the midst thereof,
like a roaring lion ravening the prey;
they have devoured souls.

EZEKIEL 22:25

We must give up the grand distinctions of
the schoolman and all the lettered technicalities
of men who have studied theology as a system
but have not felt the power of it in their hearts.

# Nearness to God

I am the door:
by me if any man enter in,
he shall be saved,
and shall go in and out,
and find pasture.

JOHN 10:9

If you love Christ, come nearer to Him,
and nearer, and nearer still.

❧

I charge you,
O daughters of Jerusalem,
if ye find my beloved, that ye tell him,
that I am sick of love.

SONG OF SOLOMON 5:8

Gracious souls are never perfectly at ease
except they are in a state of nearness to Christ;
for when they are away from Him
they lose their peace.
The nearer to Him,
the nearer to the perfect calm of heaven;
the nearer to Him,
the fuller the heart is, not only of peace,
but of life, and vigour, and joy,
for these all depend on
constant intercourse with Jesus.

# Need

And of his fulness have all we received.
JOHN 1:16

Come, believer, and get all thy need supplied; ask largely,
and thou shalt receive largely.

But my God shall supply all your need.
PHILIPPIANS 4:19

Sufficient for the day is all that we can enjoy. We cannot
eat or drink or wear more than the day's supply of food
and raiment; the surplus gives us the care of storing it,
and the anxiety of watching against a thief.

He hath given meat unto them that fear him:
he will ever be mindful of his covenant.
PSALM 111:5

In Jesus all needful things are laid up for you.

# Nonconformity

This people draweth nigh
unto me with their mouth,
and honoureth me with their lips;
but their heart is far from me.

MATTHEW 15:8

The Christian, while in the world,
is not to be of the world.
He should be distinguished from it in
the great object of his life.
To him, "to live," should be "Christ."
Whether he eats, or drinks,
or whatever he does,
he should do all to God's glory.

Be ye separate.

2 CORINTHIANS 6:17

And you should be separate from
the world in your actions.
If a thing be right,
though you lose by it, it must be done;
if it be wrong, though you would gain by it,
you must scorn the sin for your Master's sake.

# Obedience

And they buried him in
the city of David among the kings,
because he had done good in Israel,
both toward God, and toward his house.

2 CHRONICLES 24:16

I would rather obey God, than rule an empire.

Your heavenly Father. . .

MATTHEW 6:26

The obedience which God's children yield
to Him must be loving obedience.
Do not go about the service of God
as slaves to their taskmaster's toil,
but run in the way of His commands
because it is your Father's way.

Therefore shall ye observe all my statutes,
and all my judgments, and do them.

LEVITICUS 19:37

How can a man be a disciple of Christ when
he lives in open disobedience to Him?

# Parenting

Tell ye your children of it,
and let your children tell their children,
and their children another generation.

JOEL 1:3

To teach our children is a personal duty;
we cannot delegate it to Sunday school teachers,
or other friendly aids.

Bring him unto me.

MARK 9:19

Children are a precious gift from God,
but much anxiety comes with them.
They may be a great joy or a great bitterness
to their parents;
they may be filled with the Spirit of God,
or possessed with the spirit of evil.
In all cases, the Word of God gives us
one receipt for the curing of all their ills,
"Bring him unto me."

# Peacemakers

Seek peace, and pursue it.

PSALM 34:14

Our peaceableness is never to be a compact with sin,
or toleration of evil.
We must set our faces like flints against everything
which is contrary to God and His holiness:
purity being in our souls a settled matter,
we can go on to peaceableness.

Blessed are the peacemakers:
for they shall be called the children of God.

MATTHEW 5:9

Purify our minds that we may be "first pure,
then peaceable," and fortify our souls,
that our peaceableness may not lead us
into cowardice and despair,
when for Thy sake we are persecuted.

# Perseverance

Weeping may endure for a night,
but joy cometh in the morning.

PSALM 30:5

It may be all dark now,
but it will soon be light;
it may be all trial now,
but it will soon be all happiness.

. . .mighty to save.

ISAIAH 63:1

Christ's might doth not lie
in making a believer
and then leaving him to shift for himself;
but He who begins the good work carries it on;
He who imparts the
first germ of life in the dead soul,
prolongs the divine existence,
and strengthens it until it bursts
asunder every bond of sin,
and the soul leaps from earth,
perfected in glory.

# Pleasure

Shew me wherefore thou
contendest with me.

JOB 10:2

God often takes away our comforts
and our privileges in order to
make us better Christians.
He trains His soldiers,
not in tents of ease and luxury,
but by turning them out and using them
to forced marches and hard service.

He that loveth pleasure
shall be a poor man:
he that loveth wine and oil
shall not be rich.

PROVERBS 21:17

Many professed Christians spend
far too much time in amusements
which they call recreation,
but which, I fear,
is far rather a redestruction
than a recreation.

# Power of God

The bow shall be seen in the cloud.
GENESIS 9:14

When Jesus walks the waters of the sea,
how profound the calm!

Thy right hand, O LORD,
is become glorious in power:
thy right hand, O LORD,
hath dashed in pieces the enemy.

EXODUS 15:6

What we cannot do in six thousand years,
He can do in an instant.

His bow abode in strength,
and the arms of his hands were made strong
by the hands of the mighty God of Jacob.
GENESIS 49:24

There is nought that we can do
without the power of God.
All true strength comes from
"the mighty God of Jacob."

# Prayer

But I give myself unto prayer.
PSALM 109:4

Prayer must not be our chance work,
but our daily business, our habit and vocation. . . .
We must addict ourselves to prayer.

I called him,
but he gave me no answer.
SONG OF SOLOMON 5:6

The Lord, when He hath given great faith,
has been known to try it by long delayings.
He has suffered His servants' voices to
echo in their ears as from a brazen sky.

Behold, he prayeth.
ACTS 9:11

Oftentimes a poor brokenhearted one bends his knee,
but can only utter his wailing
in the language of sighs and tears;
yet that groan has made all the harps of heaven
thrill with music.

And when he had thus spoken,
he took bread,
and gave thanks to God
in presence of them all.
ACTS 27:35

It is interesting to remark
how large a portion of Sacred Writ
is occupied with the subject of prayer. . . .
We may be certain that whatever
God has made prominent in His Word,
He intended to be conspicuous in our lives.
If He has said much about prayer,
it is because He knows we have much need of it.

Pray without ceasing.
1 THESSALONIANS 5:17

Prayer can never be in excess.

Hearken unto the voice of my cry,
my King, and my God:
for unto thee will I pray.
PSALM 5:2

If there is no prayer,
you may be quite sure the soul is dead.

# Presence of God

I will never leave thee.
HEBREWS 13:5

Be thou bold to believe,
for He hath said,
"I will never leave thee,
nor forsake thee."
In this promise,
God gives to His people everything.

Isaac went out to meditate
in the field at the eventide.
GENESIS 24:63

If the business of this day will permit it,
it will be well, dear reader,
if you can spare an hour
to walk in the field at eventide,
but if not, the Lord is in the town, too,
and will meet with thee in thy chamber
or in the crowded street.
Let thy heart go forth to meet Him.

# Professing God

And they took knowledge of them,
that they had been with Jesus.

ACTS 4:13

Never blush to own your religion;
your profession will never disgrace you:
Take care you never disgrace that.

Except a man be born again,
he cannot see the kingdom of God.

JOHN 3:3

Be ye quite assured that
the name of a Christian
is not the nature of a Christian,
and that your being born in a Christian land
and being recognized as professing
the Christian religion is of no avail
whatever unless there be
something more added to it—
the being born again
as a subject of Jesus Christ.

# Promises

He is not here:
for he is risen, as he said.
Come, see the place where the Lord lay.

MATTHEW 28:6

Jesus always keeps His word:
"He is risen, as he said."
He said He would rise from the dead,
and He did;
He says that His people also shall rise,
and they shall.

Do as thou hast said.

2 SAMUEL 7:25

Think not that God will be troubled
by your importunately reminding Him
of His promises.
He loves to hear the loud outcries of needy souls.
It is His delight to bestow favours.
He is more ready to hear than you are to ask.

68

# Protection

I have prayed for thee.
LUKE 22:32

O Jesus, what a comfort it is
that thou hast pleaded our cause
against our unseen enemies;
countermined their mines,
and unmasked their ambushes.

We know that all things work together
for good to them that love God.
ROMANS 8:28

The Christian does not
merely hold this as a theory,
but he knows it as a matter of fact.
Everything has worked for good as yet;
the poisonous drugs mixed in fit proportions
have worked the cure;
the sharp cuts of the lancet
have cleansed out the proud flesh
and facilitated the healing.

# Purity

. . .perfect in Christ Jesus.

COLOSSIANS 1:28

Filthy as thou art, thou shalt be clean.

Who can say,
I have made my heart clean,
I am pure from my sin?

PROVERBS 20:9

Christ takes a worm
and transforms it into an angel.

Many shall be purified,
and made white, and tried;
but. . .none of the wicked shall understand.

DANIEL 12:10

There is not an ingot of silver
in heaven's treasury which has not been
in the furnace on earth
and been purified seven times. . . .
If you are a servant of the Lord,
you must be tried "as gold is tried."

# Salvation

Say unto my soul,
I am thy salvation.

PSALM 35:3

Let me have a present, personal, infallible,
indisputable sense that I am Thine,
and that Thou art mine.

Neither is there salvation in any other.

ACTS 4:12

Jesus will never be a part-saviour.

Without faith it is impossible to please him.

HEBREWS 11:6

There never was a man who
could walk into salvation erect.
We must go to Christ on our bended knees;
for though He is a door big enough for
the greatest sinner to come in,
He is a door so low that men must
stoop if they would be saved.

# Sin

All these evil things come from within,
and defile the man.

MARK 7:23

Beware of light thoughts of sin.

Sin. . .exceeding sinful.

ROMANS 7:13

Sin, a little thing? Is it not a poison?
. . .Do not little strokes fell lofty oaks?
Will not continual droppings wear away stones?

Know ye not that a little leaven
leaveneth the whole lump?

1 CORINTHIANS 5:6

A little filth acquired every day,
if it be left unwashed,
will make us as black as if
we had been plunged in the mire.

He shall save his people
from their sins.

MATTHEW 1:21

Christ saves His people,
not in their sins,
but from them.

For they loved the praise of men more than
the praise of God.

JOHN 12:43

Sympathy in sin is conspiracy in crime.

Keep back thy servant also
from presumptuous sins;
let them not have dominion over me:
then shall I be upright,
and I shall be innocent from
the great transgression.

PSALM 19:13

There is a natural proneness
to sin in the best of men,
and they must be held back
as a horse is held back
by the bit or they will run into it.

# Sorrow

The things which are not seen. . .
2 CORINTHIANS 4:18

The joys of heaven will surely
compensate for the sorrows of earth.

He was sore athirst,
and called on the LORD, and said,
Thou hast given this great deliverance
into the hand of thy servant:
and now shall I die for thirst?
JUDGES 15:18

The road of sorrow is the road to heaven,
but there are wells of refreshing water
all along the route.

Take up the cross, and follow me.
MARK 10:21

Jesus was a cross-bearer;
He leads the way in the path of sorrow.

# Soul-Winning

For thou shalt be his witness unto all men
of what thou hast seen and heard.

ACTS 22:15

Soul-winning is the chief business of
the Christian minister;
indeed, it should be the main pursuit
of every true believer.

Provide neither gold, nor silver,
nor brass in your purses.

MATTHEW 10:9

A soul-winner can do
nothing without God. . . .
Dependence upon God is
our strength and our joy:
in that dependence let us go forth
and seek to win souls for Him.

# Sovereignty

I will cut off. . .
them that worship and
that swear by the LORD,
and that swear by Malcham.

ZEPHANIAH 1:4–5

To have one foot on the land of truth,
and another on the sea of falsehood,
will involve a terrible fall and a total ruin.
Christ will be all or nothing.
God fills the whole universe,
and hence there is no room for another god.

Give unto the LORD
the glory due unto his name.

PSALM 29:2

The moment we glorify ourselves,
since there is room for
one glory only in the universe,
we set ourselves up as rivals to the Most High.
Shall the insect of an hour glorify itself
against the sun which warmed it into life?
Shall the potsherd exalt itself above the man
who fashioned it upon the wheel?

76

I remember thee.

JEREMIAH 2:2

When the world was set upon its pillars,
He was there,
and He set the bounds of the people
according to the number of the children of Israel.

Oh that I were as in months past.

JOB 29:2

A jealous God will not be content
with a divided heart;
He must be loved first and best.
He will withdraw the sunshine of His presence
from a cold, wandering heart.

How canst thou say,
I am not polluted,
I have not gone after Baalim?

JEREMIAH 2:23

Jehovah and Baal can never be friends.
"Ye cannot serve God and Mammon."
"No man can serve two masters."
All attempts at compromise in matters of truth
and purity are founded on falsehood.

# Spirit

And they were all filled with
the Holy Ghost.
ACTS 2:4

As the wind, He brings the breath of life to men;
blowing where He listeth
He performs the quickening operations
by which the spiritual creation is
animated and sustained.

Thy good spirit. . .
NEHEMIAH 9:20

Common, too common is
the sin of forgetting the Holy Spirit.

In whom ye also are builded together for an
habitation of God through the Spirit.
EPHESIANS 2:22

The church will never prosper until
more reverently it believes
in the Holy Ghost.

It is the spirit that quickeneth;
the flesh profiteth nothing.

JOHN 6:63

You might sit at a thousand Sacraments,
and you might be baptized in a myriad of pools,
but all this would not avail one jot or tittle
for your salvation unless you had the spirit
that quickened you.

The trees of the LORD are full of sap.

PSALM 104:16

The mere name of being a Christian is
but a dead thing;
we must be filled with
the spirit of divine life.

Grieve not the holy Spirit.

EPHESIANS 4:30

Are you wanting to be made
like the angels of God,
full of zeal and ardour for the Master's cause?
You cannot without the Spirit—
"Without me ye can do nothing."

# Suffering

Though he were a Son,
yet learned he obedience
by the things which he suffered.
HEBREWS 5:8

Our Master's experience teaches us
that suffering is necessary,
and the true-born child of God must not,
would not, escape it if he might.

For as the sufferings of Christ abound in us,
so our consolation also aboundeth by Christ.
2 CORINTHIANS 1:5

It is a blessed thing,
that when we are most cast down,
then it is that we are most lifted up
by the consolations of the Spirit.

But rejoice, inasmuch as ye are
partakers of Christ's sufferings.
1 PETER 4:13

Great hearts can only be made by great troubles.

# Temptation

And it came to pass in an eveningtide,
that David arose from off his bed,
and walked upon the roof of the king's house.

2 SAMUEL 11:2

At that hour David saw Bathsheba.
We are never out of the reach of temptation.
Both at home and abroad we are liable
to meet with allurements to evil.

Then was Jesus led up of the Spirit into
the wilderness to be tempted of the devil.

MATTHEW 4:1

A holy character does not avert temptation—
Jesus was tempted.
When Satan tempts us,
his sparks fall upon tinder;
but in Christ's case,
it was like striking sparks on water;
yet the enemy continued his evil work.

Ye are Christ's.

1 CORINTHIANS 3:23

When tempted to sin, reply,
"I cannot do this great wickedness,
for I am Christ's."

∽

Be sober, be vigilant.

1 PETER 5:8

Like the old knights in wartime,
we must sleep with helmet
and breastplate buckled on,
for the arch-deceiver will seize
our first unguarded hour to make us his prey.

∽

I will take heed to my ways.

PSALM 39:1

The road is very miry;
it will be hard to pick your path
so as not to soil your garments.
This is a world of pitch;
you will need to watch often,
if in handling it
you are to keep your hands clean.

# Treachery

Betrayest thou the Son of man with a kiss?

LUKE 22:48

Whenever a man is about to stab religion,
he usually professes very great reverence for it.

Evening wolves. . .

HABAKKUK 1:8

False teachers who craftily and industriously
hunt for the precious life,
devouring men by their falsehoods,
are as dangerous and detestable
as evening wolves.

Lead me, O LORD, in thy righteousness
because of mine enemies.

PSALM 5:8

Not only are we under surveillance,
but there are more spies than we reckon of.
The espionage is everywhere,
at home and abroad.

# Trials

Let not your heart be troubled:
ye believe in God, believe also in me.

JOHN 14:1

Jesus did not pray that you should
be taken out of the world,
and what He did not pray
for you need not desire.
Better far in the Lord's strength
to meet the difficulty,
and glorify Him in it.

He led them forth by the right way.

PSALM 107:7

The eclipse of your faith,
the darkness of your mind,
the fainting of your hope,
all these things are but parts of God's method
of making you ripe for the great inheritance
upon which you shall soon enter.

# Triumph

Nay, in all these things
we are more than conquerors
through him that loved us.

ROMANS 8:37

You must be conquerors through Him
who hath loved you, if conquerors at all.

But thanks be to God,
which giveth us the victory
through our Lord Jesus Christ.

1 CORINTHIANS 15:57

If you ever try to fight
with sin in your own strength,
or on a legal footing,
or because you feel that
you will be condemned if
you do not overcome those sins,
you will be as weak as water.
The manner of victory is
through the blood of the Lamb.

He hath delivered my soul
in peace from the battle.

PSALM 55:18

The Christian's battlefield is here,
but the triumphal procession is above.

For, lo, I will command,
and I will sift the house of Israel
among all nations,
like as corn is sifted in a sieve,
yet shall not the least grain
fall upon the earth.

AMOS 9:9

Thou shalt have the brightest part
of the victory if thou art in
the fiercest of the conflict.

I am come that they might have life,
and that they might have it more abundantly.

JOHN 10:10

As long as there is a God,
the believer shall not only exist, but live.

# Trust

They looked unto him, and were lightened:
and their faces were not ashamed.

PSALM 34:5

You are not to be your own physician
and then go to Christ,
but go just as you are;
the only salvation for you is to trust
implicitly, simply, nakedly, on Christ.

But whosoever drinketh of
the water that I shall give him
shall never thirst;
but the water that I shall give him
shall be in him a well of water
springing up into everlasting life.

JOHN 4:14

A man may starve with bread
upon the table if he does not eat,
and he may perish with thirst
though he be up to his neck in water
if he does not drink.
Have you trusted Christ?

# Unbelief

For all this they sinned still,
and believed not for his wondrous works.
PSALM 78:32

Unbelief hath more phases than
the moon and more colors than the chameleon.

And that lord answered the man of God,
and said, Now, behold,
if the LORD should make windows in heaven,
might such a thing be?
And he said,
Behold, thou shalt see it with thine eyes,
but shalt not eat thereof.
2 KINGS 7:19

Not to believe nullifies everything.
It is the fly in the ointment;
it is the poison in the pot.

And he marvelled because of their unbelief.
MARK 6:6

Do you not know that unbelief kept
Moses and Aaron out of Canaan?

How long will it be ere they believe me?

NUMBERS 14:11

Strive with all diligence to keep out
that monster unbelief.
It so dishonours Christ,
that He will withdraw His visible presence
if we insult Him by indulging it.

Afterward he appeared unto the eleven. . .
and upbraided them with their unbelief
and hardness of heart.

MARK 16:14

The moment you cease to believe,
that moment distress comes in,
and down you go.

If ye will not believe,
surely ye shall not be established.

ISAIAH 7:9

Unbelief not only begets,
but fosters sin.

# Wealth

Your riches are corrupted.
JAMES 5:2

God has been very merciful to some of us
in never letting money come rolling in upon us,
for most men are carried off their legs
if they meet with a great wave of fortune.

❧

Lay not up for yourselves
treasures upon earth,
where moth and rust doth corrupt,
and where thieves break through and steal.
MATTHEW 6:19

May none of us ever be affected by
considerations of profit and loss
in matters of doctrine, matters of duty,
and matters of right and wrong!

❧

Go to now, ye rich men, weep and howl
for your miseries that shall come upon you.
JAMES 5:1

It is a dangerous thing to be prosperous.
The crucible of adversity is a less severe trial to
the Christian than the fining-pot of prosperity.

# Will of God

Jesus saith unto them,
My meat is to do the will of him that sent me,
and to finish his work.

JOHN 4:34

Leave not thy chamber this morning
without enquiring of the Lord.

And. . .David enquired of the LORD.

2 SAMUEL 5:23

Learn from David to take no step without God.

Jehoshaphat made ships of Tharshish
to go to Ophir for gold:
but they went not;
for the ships were broken at Ezion-geber.

1 KINGS 22:48

Providence prospers one,
and frustrates the desires of another,
in the same business and at the same spot,
yet the Great Ruler is as good and wise
at one time as another.

# Wisdom

Lead me in thy truth, and teach me:
for thou art the God of my salvation;
on thee do I wait all the day.

PSALM 25:5

It were well for many professors if
instead of following their own devices,
and cutting out new paths
of thought for themselves,
they would enquire for the good old ways
of God's own truth,
and beseech the Holy Ghost
to give them sanctified understandings
and teachable spirits.

Who of God is made unto us wisdom.

1 CORINTHIANS 1:30

The temptation with a man of
refined thought and high education is
to depart from the simple truth
of Christ crucified,
and to invent, as the term is,
a more intellectual doctrine.

# Word of God

Then opened he their understanding,
that they might understand the scriptures.

LUKE 24:45

Let us sit at the feet of Jesus,
and by earnest prayer call in His blessed aid
that our dull wits may grow brighter,
and our feeble understandings
may receive heavenly things.

The liberty wherewith Christ hath made us free.

GALATIANS 5:1

Scripture is a never-failing treasury filled with
boundless stories of grace.
It is the bank of heaven;
you may draw from it as much as you please.

He hath said.

HEBREWS 13:5

Should you not, besides reading the Bible,
store your memories richly
with the promises of God?

# Work

He did it with all his heart, and prospered.

2 CHRONICLES 31:21

The Holy Spirit helps our infirmities,
but He does not encourage our idleness;
He loves active believers.

&

Whatsoever thy hand findeth to do,
do it with thy might.

ECCLESIASTES 9:10

We need workshop faith,
as well as prayer-meeting faith.

&

And he goeth up into a mountain,
and calleth unto him whom he would:
and they came unto him.

MARK 3:13

This morning we must endeavour
to ascend the mount of communion,
that there we may be ordained to the
lifework for which we are set apart.
Let us not see the face of man today
till we have seen Jesus.

# *Worry*

The lot is cast into the lap;
but the whole disposing thereof is of the LORD.

PROVERBS 16:33


You are meddling with Christ's business,
and neglecting your own when you
fret about your lot and circumstances.
You have been trying "providing" work
and forgetting that it is yours to obey.
Be wise and attend to the obeying,
and let Christ manage the providing.

Therefore I say unto you,
Take no thought for your life,
what ye shall eat,
or what ye shall drink;
nor yet for your body,
what ye shall put on.
Is not the life more than meat,
and the body than raiment?

MATTHEW 6:25


If God cares for you, why need you care, too?
Can you trust Him for your soul,
and not for your body?

# Worship

Who shall not fear thee, O Lord,
and glorify thy name?

REVELATION 15:4

Mechanical worship is easy,
but worthless.

Give unto the LORD the glory
due unto his name.

PSALM 96:8

God was at the prayer-meeting. . . .
God doesn't bless empty seats.

God is a Spirit:
and they that worship him must
worship him in spirit and in truth.

JOHN 4:24

When people come merely to hear a minister,
or for custom's sake, or for form's sake,
do they not always get what they come for?